The Witch Princess

Jim Alderson

Stanley Thornes (Publishers) Ltd

© Jim Alderson 1987

All rights reserved. No part of this publication may be reproduced or transmitted in any form or by any means, electronic or mechanical, including photocopy, recording, or any information storage and retrieval system, without permission in writing from the publisher or under licence from the Copyright Licensing Agency Limited. Further details of such licences (for reprographic reproduction) may be obtained from the Copyright Licensing Agency Limited, of 90 Tottenham Court Road, London W1P 9HE.

First published in 1977 by Hutchinson Education
Reprinted in 1979, 1982, 1989

Reprinted in 1992 by
Stanley Thornes (Publishers) Ltd
Old Station Drive
Leckhampton
CHELTENHAM GL53 0DN
England

ISBN 0 7487 1048 5

Cover photograph by Steve Richards
Cover design by Ned Hoste
Printed and bound in Great Britain at Martin's of Berwick

1

Peter was a Russian boy. He was the son of a woodcutter. He was poor but happy. Then his father died. His father was crushed by a falling tree. The body was put into a coffin. The next day it was taken to a graveyard. Peter went there with his grandfather.

The boy watched the coffin being covered with earth. His father was buried next to his mother. Now both Peter's parents were dead. Peter began to cry. It was the first time he had ever cried in his life. What would happen to him now?

A man came over to him. It was one of his uncles. 'I have found you a job,' said the uncle. 'You are very lucky indeed. You will work in the King's palace. You will be a servant there. You must go there tomorrow.'

The uncle walked away. Peter was not happy. He did not like his uncle. He did not want to leave his grandfather. The old man had tears in his eyes.

'Goodbye, Peter,' he said. 'Be careful. The King is a strange and cruel man. Some say he is mad. One moment he will laugh and joke with you, and the next moment he will cut off your head. He has a daughter. She is his only child. There is something odd about her too. People say there is a curse on her. You must take care. If anything happens, come and see me. I might be able to help. I am old but I am wise.'

A black horse was sent to fetch Peter. He was taken to the King's palace. It was a huge place. There were parks and gardens all around it. Peter got off the horse. He was very nervous. He felt all alone. What was the King like? Was he mad? What was the King's daughter like? Why did people say there was a curse on her?

2

Peter was shown into a room. It was the biggest room he had ever seen. There were thick carpets everywhere. The walls were covered with beautiful paintings.

The King was near a window. He was sitting on a chair of gold. When he saw Peter, he got up. Peter was afraid. The King had a long white beard just like Father Christmas, but his eyes were cruel.

'Are you the woodcutter's son?' asked the King. 'Yes, your majesty,' said Peter. 'Good,' said the King. 'You are now my servant. You are very lucky to be here. You will look after my daughter, and obey her in everything. Do you understand?' 'Yes, your majesty.'

'Good,' said the King. He laughed. 'If you do not do as you are told, you will be thrown to my wolves. They are always hungry. Poor things!' He laughed again.

Peter shook with fear. He knew the King was not joking. He knew his grandfather was right. The King was a cruel madman. 'Come with me,' said the King. 'I will show you my daughter.'

The King took Peter into another big room. The princess had her back to them. She was looking into the fire. 'Catherine,' said the King. 'This is your new servant. His name is Peter.'

The girl turned around. She had long blond hair and blue eyes. She was very beautiful. But there was something odd about her. Peter did not know what it was, but she gave him the creeps.

She came over and held out her hand. Peter kissed it. He shivered. Her hand was as cold as ice. She began to laugh. It was an odd sort of laugh. Perhaps she was mad too, thought Peter. 'I hope you will be happy here,' she said. Then she went back to the fire.

Peter was shown to his room. He was very tired, but did not get much sleep that night. He could see the King outside. The man kept looking up at the moon and walking about. The moon seemed to pull him along like a magnet. It was all very strange.

After a while Peter began to hear strange noises. They were coming from the room beside him. He could hear hissing and scratching. There was a smell too. As if something was burning. Peter trembled. What was it? What was going on?

3

The next morning Peter got up very early. He went into the garden. He wanted to get some fresh air. He found a ball. He began to throw it against the side of a wall.

It was a beautiful day. The sun was shining. Birds were singing in the trees. Bees were humming in and out of the flowers. A small dog came out of a kennel and began to play with him.

Suddenly he felt cold. He shivered. Something was wrong. The birds stopped singing. The dog ran away with its tail between its legs. Even the bees stopped humming. He turned round to see what it was. It was the princess!

Peter was frightened of her. He did not know why. After all she was only a girl of his own age, even though she was a princess. She did not say anything. She just stood there. Her eyes looked strange. Peter felt she was trying to put a spell on him.

She moved closer. It began to get colder. She picked up the ball and placed it in Peter's hands. Her touch was as cold as ice. Peter began to shiver. 'What is the matter?' she said. 'Your hands are cold,' he said.

She smiled. Then she said something very odd. 'It is very hot where I come from,' she said. 'I have to fly about at night to cool down. I have been to the moon, and I have slept on the stars.' Then she bent down to pick up a piece of rock.

Peter moved away from her. She was crazy too! She was as mad as a hatter. He did not like the way she held the rock in her hands.

'Shall I tell you how to stay alive?' she said. Peter nodded his head. She smiled and showed her teeth. 'You must stay in your room at night,' she said.

Then she began to squeeze the rock in her hands. Peter stared at her. He just could not believe it. She was crushing the rock in her bare hands. She crushed it to powder, then she walked away.

Peter shook his head. It was like a bad dream. He had read somewhere that mad people were as strong as ten normal men.

He felt trapped. That day Peter worked hard. He cleaned all the princess's shoes and took her all her meals. He washed the dishes, scrubbed the tables and did hundreds of other little jobs. At the end of the day he felt worn out. He wanted to get a good night's sleep.

But that night it all started again. The King went out for his walk and Peter could hear the strange sounds again. They were coming from the room at the side. He knew by now that this was the room of the princess.

He felt lonely and scared. The strange noises began to get louder and louder. He could hear scratching and hissing again. There was the same smell of burning.

Peter wanted to go and have a look, but he was too scared. He kept thinking of what the princess had said. She had said, 'If you want to stay alive you must stay in your room at night.'

The strange noises kept getting louder and louder. Peter got up off his bed. He could not stand it any longer. He was going to see what it was all about.

5

Peter opened his door. The sound of hissing grew louder. It was coming from the princess's room. He got down on his knees and looked through the keyhole. He could not believe what he saw!

The princess had her back to him. She was kneeling in front of the fire. She was hissing and growling. She kept putting her arms into the air and saying, 'Come, my master. Come to me.' Then she scratched the floor and hissed again.

Smoke was coming out of the fire. It filled the room. Suddenly a strange shape began to appear. Slowly it took form. It had horns and evil-looking eyes. It grew larger and larger. The princess began to scream. It was a scream of joy. 'My master!' she said.

Then the boy saw a terrible thing happen. The princess kept her back to him but her head began to twist around. He could not believe it. Her body was facing one way and her head was facing the other way. No human being could do that. He knew then that the princess was some kind of witch.

Peter did not wait to see any more. He ran back to his room. Then he locked the door. His heart was thumping like a hammer.

Suddenly there was a scratching noise at the door. He could hear a strange, hissing voice. It was the princess.

'Peter,' she said. 'You did not listen to my warning. Now you know my secret. You must die. I will tear you to pieces. Nothing can save you. I will enjoy killing you.' Then Peter heard the mad laughter of the King from behind the door. Next moment he fainted.

6

The next day the princess became very ill. She told everyone she was dying. The King was very upset. He started to cry. Even though he was a very cruel man, he loved his daughter.

The princess reached out her hand. She touched the King on the arm. 'Father,' she said. 'I will die soon. Will you promise to do something for me?'

The man took her hand. Tears were running down his face. 'Yes,' he said. 'I promise. You are all I have left in the world. You are my angel sent from heaven.'

The princess smiled to herself. Her father did not know the truth. What a fool he was! 'When I die,' said the princess, 'you must put my body in a coffin. Then you must put the coffin inside the old church on top of the hill.'

The princess sat up and grabbed her father's hands. 'I want you to make Peter sit alone by my coffin for three days and three nights. I want him to pray for me, so that my soul will go to heaven when I die. Please promise me, father! I am so frightened of dying. Please promise me!'

'I promise,' said the King. 'Promise on the Bible,' said the princess. The King did as he was told. He was like a puppet. It was as if she had put a spell on him.

The next moment she said, 'I am going, father. Goodbye. Remember your promise.' Then she closed her eyes. She was dead.

The King sat down and wept. Ten minutes later he sent for a soldier. He told him to fetch Peter at once.

7

Peter heard a knock at the door of his room. He went to see who it was. There stood the soldier. 'What do you want?' asked Peter. 'The King wants to see you,' said the man.

'Why?' asked the boy. The soldier was angry. 'Do not ask questions,' he said. 'The King is waiting. Do you want me to drag you there?' 'No,' said Peter. 'I will come with you.'

Peter was taken to the room of the princess. The King was waiting to meet him. Peter was very frightened.

The princess's bed was empty. A coffin stood in the middle of the room. In it lay the princess. She was dead, but there was a strange smile on her lips.

'I have a job for you,' said the King. 'My daughter is dead. Her body will be taken to the church on top of the hill. She has asked for you to pray over her coffin. You will do this for three days and three nights.'

Peter was filled with terror. He went down on his knees. 'Oh no!' he said. 'Please! Anything but that!'

The King was amazed. He did not understand. He was angry. 'What is this?' he yelled. 'Get back on your feet, you dog! You will do as I say.' 'No!' said Peter.

The King went almost mad with anger. He shouted and shook his fists. He was trembling all over. Nobody had ever said no to him before.

'You little insect!' he said. 'I will have your hands and feet cut off. I will feed you to my wolves. I will have you dropped head first into a big tank of boiling fat. Do you understand me?'

Peter nodded. There was nothing he could do. He did not dare tell the King his daughter was a witch. 'Now get out of my sight,' said the King. 'My soldier will fetch you tomorrow.'

8

Peter went slowly back to his room. He was very unhappy. The witch would come out of her coffin in the middle of the night. She would tear him to pieces. He could see her long, cruel nails ripping the skin off his back and chest. She would bite through his arms. She would tear out his eyes. She would sink her teeth into his neck and pull his head off. Russian witches were the worst witches in the world!

Peter sat down on his bed. He held his head in his hands. There was no hope for him. If he did not watch over the coffin, he would be fed to the wolves or boiled in oil. That was almost as bad as being killed by the witch!

It was then that Peter remembered the words of his grandfather. He put on a coat and crept out of the palace. He ran across the parks and through the huge gates. He did not stop running until he reached his grandfather's hut.

9

Peter told the old man about the princess. He expected the old man to laugh. To his surprise he was very sad.

'It is a curse,' he said. 'The Devil has put a curse on the King. The princess is a witch. I have suspected that for some time.' 'What will she do to me?' asked the boy.

Grandad gave an unhappy sigh. 'The witch will come out of her coffin at midnight. She will tear all the flesh from your bones. It will be just like a butcher skinning a rabbit. When she has done this, she will wait for the Devil to come. He will come for her on a white horse, and take her straight back to Hell.

Peter was shaking with fear. 'Is there any way I can be saved?' he asked. He saw his grandad scratch his beard. 'I can help you,' he said, 'but you must listen to me very carefully. Russian witches are the worst in the world. If you make one mistake you will be dead.' 'I am listening,' said the boy.

The old man handed him a piece of chalk from a wooden box. 'Take that piece of chalk,' he said. 'When you are in the church, you must draw a circle round yourself. It must be a perfect circle. If there is the slightest gap, the witch will be able to enter. She will then be able to tear you into pieces.

You must not leave this magic circle during the night. You must stand with your back to the coffin. You must not fall asleep or turn round. The witch will torment you for three nights. She will grow stronger and more frightening every night. You will need to be very brave.'

Peter took the piece of chalk and put it in his pocket. 'Is there anything else?' he said. 'Yes,' said his grandad. 'Take this Bible. It is God's book. It will help save you from the powers of evil.' 'Thanks,' said Peter.

'May God be with you,' said his grandad, 'and be careful. The witch is full of tricks.' Peter ran all the way back to the palace.

10

Next morning there was a knock at Peter's door. This time Peter was ready. The soldier took him to the top of the hill. The King was waiting for them inside the church. He was standing beside a long white coffin.

'Good,' said the King. 'There is food and water on the table. It will last you three days. You will be in the church all by yourself. The door will be locked and bolted on the outside. That was what my daughter wanted. We will let you out in three days' time.'

The King and soldier walked towards the door. 'Goodbye,' said the King. 'I hope you enjoy yourself.' He laughed and slammed the door.

Peter looked down at the coffin. The lid had been nailed down very tight. But would it be strong enough to hold back the princess? No! The princess was a Russian witch. Russian witches were the worst in the world. They got their terrible power from the Devil himself

Peter had a good look at the church. It was very old and dark. There were candles on the table and some food and water. He tried to open the door but it was locked. The window above was far too high to reach. There was no escape. He was trapped.

All of a sudden Peter felt very tired. He had not slept well at all. He decided to have a short sleep. It was still early in the afternoon. Later on, he would need all his strength. Now he had to rest.

The boy fell into a deep sleep. He had all sorts of terrible dreams. Hour after hour passed by, and he did not wake up.

When evening came, shadows crept across the floor of the church. Still the boy slept on. A tiny evil-looking spider crawled up through a hole in the coffin. It stared at the boy for a few moments. Then it was gone.

After a while the moon and stars could be seen at the window. The boy did not awake. It was as if some strange power was keeping him fast asleep.

11

Suddenly an owl hooted very loudly.

The boy's eyes opened in a flash. He knew he had overslept. He was terrified. He felt in his pockets for the chalk. It was so dark he could not see. Where were his matches? A church clock began to strike outside.

One! Two!
He dropped the chalk.
Three! Four!
Was it twelve o'clock? Was it too late?
Five! Six! Seven!
He went down on his hands and knees. Where was the chalk?
Eight! Nine!
It was too late. He was as good as dead. Nothing could stop the witch now.
Ten! Eleven!
Silence. The owl hooted again. More silence.

He was saved! It was not yet twelve.

There was no time to lose. The boy found a box of matches and lit one of the candles on the table. He picked up the chalk and drew a circle around

21

himself. He went down on his knees and looked at it very carefully. There must not be the slightest gap in the circle.

When he had done this, Peter picked up the Bible. Then he stepped inside the circle. He stood with his back to the coffin. In front of him was the window. He could see the moon and the stars shining down.

He waited. Time passed very slowly. A goat made a bleating sound on a hillside. A bird sang for a few moments. Then there was silence. The candle made strange shadows on the wall and he saw a rat run into the darkness.

Suddenly the air began to get cold. He shivered. He felt as if someone had dropped ice down his neck. He knew something terrible was going to happen. The owl hooted again. The clock began to strike. It struck twelve times. It was midnight. This was the witching hour. This was the time of evil!

He waited. At first he heard nothing. He listened again. Then he heard it. A slight scratching noise. This was followed by a creaking sound. He knew that the lid was being pushed upwards. He heard the nails begin to open.

His heart began to thump madly. He wanted to run for his life. He felt like a fly trapped in a web. And the witch was like a spider. She would put her long fangs into his flesh. His knees banged together in fear.

The coffin lid clattered to the floor. He could hear the witch sniffing the air. Next there was a scream of joy. She had seen him! He heard her lips smacking together as she ran towards him.

12

All of a sudden he heard her stop. She gave a cry of rage. A terrible cry of rage. There was something stopping her from getting at him. It held her back. She rushed all around the circle yelling with anger.

Now he could see her quite clearly. She was no longer a beautiful young girl. Her face was white and twisted. Her teeth were long and sharp and cruel. Water dribbled from her mouth. She growled and rolled her eyes like a wild beast. Then she went down on her knees and looked at the circle. Was there a gap?

Peter tried not to look. He kept his eyes on the Bible. All the same, he could still see her. Now she was hissing like a snake and grunting like a pig. Suddenly she spoke. Her voice was loud and cruel.

'Peter,' she said. 'Look at me. I am one of the Devil's many daughters. Do you really think you can escape me? I will get stronger and stronger every night. You will not escape me.'

She rushed across to the table. She emptied the water on to the floor and laughed. Then she placed the food in the dust and gave a whistle. Rats came from all parts of the church. They began to eat the food. They bit each other and made angry noises.

'Now you have no food and water,' said the witch. 'You will grow weak. You will go to sleep and you will die.' She went back towards her coffin. 'I will come for you tomorrow,' she said. 'I will be stronger then.'

Peter listened to her cruel laugh. He heard the noise of the coffin lid. It was being slid back into place.

He saw the rats eat his food. He saw their huge twisted shadows on the wall. They looked like a pack of wolves ripping an animal to pieces.

13

Next morning, Peter rushed from the circle. He was frightened out of his wits. He banged upon the door, screaming and shouting. But it was no good. He could hear only one sound. It was the bleating of a goat on the hill.

Peter could not sleep. He was too frightened. He watched the sun. It rose high in the sky. Then it began to fall slowly. Long shadows began to creep across the floor of the church. The clock struck seven.

The boy walked over to the coffin. An evil looking spider came up through a hole in the lid. It watched him for a few moments. Peter was angry. This spider had been sent by the witch. It had been sent to spy on him. He tried to crush it with his shoe but it went back down the hole.

Peter wanted to find out more. He wanted to look inside the coffin. He took a deep breath. He put out his hand and touched the coffin lid. As he did so, he heard the sound of laughter. It was an evil sound. It made his blood run cold. The noise came up from the coffin. It grew louder and louder. It could be heard all round the church.

Peter took his hand away and the laughing stopped. He picked up his Bible and stepped back into the circle. It would soon be midnight again.

14

The clock struck twelve. Peter waited for the coffin lid to fall to the ground. But he could not hear a thing. There was complete silence. Then he heard the sound of a voice. It was soft and sweet. It was the voice of the princess, the voice of a young girl!

'Please help me,' it said. 'You must save me, Peter! Turn around and break the witch's spell.'

But the boy remembered the words of his grandfather. He did not turn around. He kept on reading his Bible. Then a white shape appeared in front of him. He looked up. His mouth fell open with shock. It really was the princess! She was even more beautiful than when he had first met her. There were tears in her eyes. She held out her hands to him.

'Peter,' she said. 'You must help me. Make a gap in your circle so I can join you there. You can always close the gap with your chalk afterwards. Act quickly before the witch awakes. There is no time to lose.'

The boy shook his head. 'No!' he said. 'I do not trust you.' He carried on reading his Bible. 'Peter!' she cried out. 'Look!'

Two more shapes appeared in front of his eyes. Peter looked up again. It was his own father and mother! He knew they were both dead, but they looked so lifelike and real! 'Peter,' said his father. 'You must let us in the circle quickly. We were not killed. We escaped. Let us in quickly or the witch will get us.'

Tears began to run down the boy's face. He had loved his parents very much. Now his mother began to cry. She sounded so sad and afraid. 'Please let me in, Peter,' she begged. 'I do not want to die. Please help me. Give me your hand. Help me over the circle.'

The boy was so upset he did not know what he was doing. He stepped to the edge of the circle. He simply had to save his parents.

Then he stopped. He did not know why, but he did. His mother kept crying out his name and his father was praying on his knees. The princess kept watching him all the time. Her eyes never left the boy's face.

Peter felt a cold shiver run down his back. He knew something was wrong. A voice in his head said, 'Be careful. The witch is full of tricks.' 'No!' he cried. 'No! Go away. You are not real!'

His mother gave a long scream, then suddenly

vanished. His father vanished as well. Peter looked towards the princess. Her face was still beautiful, but now it was filled with hate. Very slowly that beautiful face began to change. The eyes became large and ugly, the teeth became sharp and evil. It had all been a trick. The witch began to hiss and licked her pointed teeth.

'I will come again tomorrow,' she said. 'I will be so powerful that nothing will be able to stop me. My master, the Devil, will be here. All the forces of Hell will be with me. Your circle will not protect you. Your grandad is one of my servants. He has tricked you into standing over my coffin. I have enjoyed watching you suffer. I like to fill my victims with terror. I like to watch them trapped like flies in a spider's web. But tomorrow you will die. I will tear you to pieces. You will wish you had never been born!'

The witch gave a dreadful laugh and rushed out of sight. Peter knew she had gone back into her coffin. He knew she was sliding the coffin lid back into place. But she did it so quietly he could not hear a sound.

15

When morning came, Peter ran out of the circle. He banged on the door and screamed and shouted. He even tried to climb up the walls of the church. But kept falling back with his fingers torn and bleeding. It was no good. There was no escape.

Peter watched the sun rise up in the sky. Then he watched it fall. Soon it had gone out of sight. He lit a candle. His hand was trembling. Would he ever see the sun again?

The boy was tired, hungry and thirsty. He sat down and stared at the coffin. Tears came into his eyes. Somehow he did not think he was going to live to see the next morning.

As he sat there, the spider came out of the coffin. Once again it stared at him. Then it moved its front two legs up and down as if to make fun of him. Peter found himself shaking. He hated spiders. He tried to crush it but it escaped back into the coffin.

Peter tried something else. This time he was going to take off the lid. His hand shook as he reached out for the wooden top. The laughter grew louder and louder.

He pushed back the lid. The church became filled with terrible screams. Then there was silence.

Peter stared down at the witch. Her eyes were open. She was watching him. She was smiling. It was a horrible smile. Her lips moved and he saw her teeth crunch together. A green slime began to dribble from her mouth and run down the side of her chin. Her fingers kept jerking and the spider was crawling slowly across her neck.

Peter slammed the lid back. It was awful! He wanted to be sick. This was the thing that would come for him during the night! This could be his last day on earth.

16

Night came. Stars began to shine through the window. Suddenly the candles began to flicker. A cold wind was beginning to blow through the church. It grew stronger and stronger. Then the candle went out. There was nothing but darkness.

Peter closed his eyes in terror. Despite the wind he could hear the clock strike twelve. Behind him, the coffin began to glow with a strange light. The witch jumped out. Now she was at her strongest. She was shining with a terrible brightness.

She began to scream. The noise was so loud that Peter's ear drums felt as if they would burst. She began to run from one side of the church to the other. She was shining like the moon. Next she was flying through the air. She was twisting and turning like a snake.

'Peter!' she cried. 'Prepare to die. The power of Hell is mine to command. I will send demons. They will break into your circle and drag you to me. Run while you have a chance!'

Two demons suddenly appeared from the shadows. They moved towards him growling and grunting.

The witch laughed louder and louder. 'Run! Run! Run!' she screamed.

The demons crossed the circle. The boy gave a scream. He could feel their breath upon his neck. A claw scraped past his chin.

'Bring him to me!' yelled the witch. They tried to pull him away. They tried as hard as they could but their hands were pushed back by a magic power. Peter took a deep breath. They could cross the circle but they could not harm him. He was safe.

The witch stopped laughing. There was fear in her eyes. She waved her claw-like hand and the demons went away. 'Very well,' said the witch. 'Now I am going to use my full powers. I will call upon my master, the Devil. He can see into your heart. He will tell me of your weakness. He knows what you fear the most.'

There was silence. The witch waited. Peter held his breath. He was beginning to sweat with horror. He could hear the sound of hoofbeats. The wind began to howl. Thunder began to roar through the sky and the walls of the church shook as if they might fall down.

A flash of lightning lit up the window. A huge face stared down upon the witch and the boy. It had the eyes of an evil goat. Horns grew from its head. 'My master!' cried the witch.

The Devil nodded. He said nothing but the sound of his breath filled the church. The air became foul with the smell of death. Peter began to feel sick. It was like some dreadful nightmare come true. The Devil's eyes seemed to go right through him. The witch was now smiling. She was getting strength from the Devil.

A thick mist rose up from the floor of the church. Peter sniffed. There was a strange evil smell. Sweat began to run down the boy's back. He started to shake all over. The shape he dreaded was moving slowly towards him through the mist. The witch grinned. It was the thing Peter feared most in all the world. It was a giant spider!

Peter stepped backwards towards the edge of the circle. The monster rushed behind him. It made sucking noises. Peter was so terrified that he almost turned around. Then the insect crossed the circle.

Again the witch screamed with laughter. Peter put his fingers in his ears. He saw the six eyes of the spider fixed on his neck. Two legs reached out for his neck. He saw the two huge fangs rise upwards. Next moment they were swaying towards him.

'Run! Run! Run!' cried the witch. But Peter did not run. He trembled and called, but he stood his ground.

The spider vanished. The wind stopped howling. A cock crowed and the sun began to peep over the hills. The witch stood still. Then she turned to the huge face at the window.

'Take me with you,' she begged. But the Devil shook his head and vanished. The sound of hoofbeats could be heard again. The Devil had gone. He had no more time for the witch, once she had failed.

The witch gave a long, low moan. She went back to the coffin and pulled on the lid. Peter waited until the sun came shining through the window. He waited till a robin started to sing. Then he fainted.

17

The King opened the church door. He saw Peter lying on the floor. He kicked the boy and shouted. 'Get up you lazy fellow. Get out of my sight. You were told to stand guard over the coffin!'

Peter got up. 'I have something to tell you,' he said. 'What is it?' asked the King. 'Your daughter is a witch,' said Peter.

'What?' yelled the King. He stamped his feet, and shook his fists with rage. 'I will have your heart cut out for saying that. I will have your burned alive. I will have you . . . .'

'Look in the coffin!' said Peter. 'Please!' He was crying. He fell down at the King's feet. 'If I am lying you may do anything you like with me.'

The King folded his arms. 'Very well,' he said. Then he turned to the soldier. 'Open the box,' he ordered. The soldier did as he was told. He pulled off the lid and looked inside. He could hardly believe his eyes. 'Good God,' he said. 'It's true.'

'What's that?' cried the King. 'Let me look.' He pushed

the soldier to one side and saw for himself.

There was the witch. Her eyes were open but she could not speak. Her lips trembled and green slime ran from the corners of her mouth. The spider was crawling across her forehead. There was fear and hate in her eyes. Her hands shook. If only it were midnight! She would then be able to tear her own father into ribbons! The King was sick. 'Get the hammer and the stake,' he said.

Moments later, the soldier returned. He placed a pointed piece of wood against the witch's heart. Then he lifted a wooden hammer and hit the stake as hard as he could.

The witch gave one of the most terrible screams that had ever been heard. The walls of the church seemed to shake. The window smashed into thousands of pieces. The witch began to twist and turn. She looked like an insect that has been stabbed through with a needle. More green slime came rushing from her mouth. Her head rolled from side to side.

Suddenly, her whole body gave one last jerk. Then she lay still. She was dead. Her claw-like hands were fixed to the stake and her eyes stared up at the roof. Peter was safe.

The King gave Peter as much money as he needed. The woodcutter's son thanked him and went away to thank his grandfather for saving him from the witch. The King died soon after. In the years to come, Peter got married. His wife was beautiful and his three childen loved him very much.

When he was an old man, he would sit his grandchildren in front of the fire. He would give them sweets and cake. Then he would tell them his true story, the story of the witch princess.

A complete list of Spirals

Stories

Jim Alderson
Crash in the Jungle
The Witch Princess

Jan Carew
Death Comes to the Circus

Susan Duberley
The Ring

Keith Fletcher and Susan Duberley
Nightmare Lake

John Goodwin
Dead-end Job

Paul Groves
Not that I'm Work-shy
The Third Climber

Anita Jackson
The Actor
The Austin Seven
Bennet Manor
Dreams
The Ear
A Game of Life or Death
No Rent to Pay

Paul Jennings
Eye of Evil
Maggot

Margaret Loxton
The Dark Shadow

Patrick Nobes
Ghost Writer

Kevin Philbin
Summer of the Werewolf

John Townsend
Beware of the Morris Minor
Fame and Fortune
SOS

David Walke
Dollars in the Dust

Plays

Jan Carew
Computer Killer
No Entry
Time Loop

John Godfrey
When I Count to Three

Nigel Gray
An Earwig in the Ear

Paul Groves
Tell Me Where it Hurts

Barbara Mitchelhill
Punchlines
The Ramsbottoms at Home

Madeline Sotheby
Hard Times at Batwing Hall

John Townsend
Cheer and Groan
The End of the Line
Hanging by a Fred
The Lighthouse Keeper's Secret
Making a Splash
Murder at Muckleby Manor
Over and Out
Rocking the Boat
Taking the Plunge

David Walke
The Bungle Gang Strikes Again
The Good, the Bad and the Bungle
Package Holiday